The Cooking with Whiskey

Whiskey Recipes That Will Blow Your Mind

BY: Allie Allen

COOK & ENJOY

Copyright 2019 Allie Allen

Copyright Notes

This book is written as an informational tool. While the author has taken every precaution to ensure the accuracy of the information provided therein, the reader is warned that they assume all risk when following the content. The author will not be held responsible for any damages that may occur as a result of the readers' actions.

The author does not give permission to reproduce this book in any form, including but not limited to: print, social media posts, electronic copies or photocopies, unless permission is expressly given in writing.

My Gift to You for Buying My Book!

I would like to extend an exclusive offer to receive free and discounted eBooks every day! This special gift is my way of saying thanks. If you fill in the subscription box below you will begin to receive special offers directly to your email.

Not only that! You will also receive notifications letting you know when an offer will expire. You will never miss a chance to get a free book! Who wouldn't want that?

Fill in the subscriber information below and get started today!

https://allie-allen.getresponsepages.com/

Table of Contents

How to Make Food with Whiskey 6

1) Whiskey Shrimp Flambé 7

2) Whiskey Three-Bean Bake 9

3) Whiskey Orange Chipotle Chicken 12

4) Whiskey Sausages 14

5) Whiskey Stout Yam Waffles 16

6) Filet Mignon with Sweet Whiskey-Coffee Sauce 18

7) Whiskey Bread Pudding 20

8) Whiskey Corn Chowder 22

9) Chocolate Waffles with Whiskey Butter Sauce 24

10) Whiskey Soda Bread 27

11) Whiskey Burgers 29

12) Honey- Whiskey Chicken Wings 31

13) Whiskey Marinated Steak with Chimichurri Sauce 33

14) Cheddar Whiskey Fondue.. 36

15) Butternut Squash Gnocchi with Whiskey Cream Sauce. 38

16) Whiskey Barbecue Sauce.. 41

17) Bourbon Whiskey Salmon 43

18) Chocolate Whiskey Balls.. 45

19) Coconut Butter Whiskey Snowballs 47

20) Irish Whiskey Potato Green Chile Stew 49

21) Cherry Apple Whiskey Sour Popsicles 51

22) One- Pan Whiskey Flavored Pork Chops 53

23) Whiskey Candied Bacon Deviled Eggs........................ 55

24) Whiskey Fudge Brownies... 57

25) Grilled Chicken with Whiskey-Ginger Marinade.......... 59

About the Author... 62

Author's Afterthoughts.. 64

How to Make Food with Whiskey

sssssssssssssssssssssssssssssssssssssssssssss

1) Whiskey Shrimp Flambé

Who doesn't like Shrimp? Unless your allergic, this succulent Shrimp sautéed in Whiskey and topped with herbs, is best served with rice or roasted vegetables.

Yield: 4

Cooking Time: 30 minutes

List of Ingredients:

- Shrimp (1 lb., deveined)
- Heavy Cream (¼ cup)
- Lemon Juice (1 tbsp.)
- Chives (¼, crushed)
- Butter (4 tbsp.)
- Tomato (1 medium, sliced)
- Whiskey (¼ cup)
- Salt & Pepper to taste
- Pecans for Garnish

ssssssssssssssssssssssssssssssssssssssssssss

Methods:

1. Melt butter in skillet over medium heat

2. Place shrimp in pan and sauté for one minute

3. Take off burner and pour in Whiskey and add back to burner

4. Toss the pan until the flames dies down, remove the shrimp and set aside.

5. Place heavy cream and tomatoes in a saucepan, bring the heat to a medium until thickened, pour in lemon juice and season with salt and pepper

6. Drop the shrimp back into the mixture and warm in sauce

7. Plate and sprinkle chives and pecans

2) Whiskey Three-Bean Bake

What a treat! These small chocolate whiskey balls would make great appetizer for any small get together the famiy would be having, whether as a treat before the main course or after, it's a burst of delight.

Yield: 8

Cooking Time: 80 minutes

List of Ingredients:

- Onion (1, diced)
- Tomatoes (1 can)
- Tomato Paste (6 tbsp.)
- Light Brown Sugar (¼ cup)
- Salt (½ tsp.)
- Black Pepper (¼ tsp.)
- Sweet Green Pepper (1, sliced)
- Molasses (½ cup)
- Dijon Mustard (2 tbsp.)
- Bacon (2 stripes)
- Whiskey (1/3 cup)
- Black Beans (1 can, drained & rinsed)
- Red Kidney Beans (1 can, drained & rinsed)
- White Kidney Beans (1 can, drained & rinsed)

ssssssssssssssssssssssssssssssssssssssssssss

Methods:

1. Set oven to 350F

2. Fry bacon stripes in olive oil in a medium skillet until crunchy and crispy.

3. Remove the bacon from pan and drain the oil.

4. Add green peppers and onions and sauté. Slowly pour in the tomatoes, molasses, tomato paste, and Whiskey, add mustard, brown sugar, salt and pepper to that mixture

5. Bring to a boil and stir for 5 minutes

6. Crush bacon stripes in the mixture along with black beans, red kidney beans and white kidney beans

7. Stir for 2 minutes then pour into a baking pan

8. Bake in 350F heated oven for 45 minutes until hot and bubbly

9. Remove and set to cool

10. After 5 minutes, Serve & Enjoy

3) Whiskey Orange Chipotle Chicken

When it comes to flavors this chicken will provide all that and more, it is very easy to make and it gives the chicken hours or days to soak all the flavors. At the first bit you will feel as if heaven has bene here on earth all along.

Yield: 6

Cooking Time: 75 minutes

List of Ingredients:

- Orange Marmalade (1 ½ cups)
- Whiskey (1 cup)
- Cilantro (½ bunch)
- Salt (1 tbsp.)
- Black Pepper (1 tbsp.)
- Chipotle Peppers in adobo sauce (8oz, 1 can)
- Tomato Paste (6oz, 1 can)
- Garlic (4 cloves, sliced)
- Olive Oil (1/3 cup)
- 6 chicken thighs

- 6 chicken legs

ssssssssssssssssssssssssssssssssssssssssssss

Methods:

1. Blend Olive Oil, Cilantro, Salt, Black Pepper, Garlic, Tomato Paste, Whiskey, Orange Marmalade, Chipotle Peppers and Adobo Sauce

2. Pour this mixture on the thighs and legs and let it marinade for 9hrs to 2 days.

3. Set oven to 400F

4. Lay the meat on baking tray cover with the chicken marinade and bake for 1 hour

5. Plate, serve and enjoy!

4) Whiskey Sausages

Succulent smoked sausage mixed in a sweet and tangy whiskey sauce, perfect for any appetizer it's usually served on toothpicks and can be eaten with rolls or bread sticks. Or on a kebab stick with an arrangement of chopped onions and sweet pepper.

Yield: 20

Cooking Time: 105 minutes

List of Ingredients:

- Whiskey (½ cup)
- Onions (¼ cup, dices)
- Ketchup (1 ¼ cups)
- Brown Sugar (½ cup)
- Dried Oregano (2 tsp.)
- Smoked Sausage (2lbs)

sssssssssssssssssssssssssssssssssssssssssssssss

Methods:

1. Set oven to 325 F. Chop smoked sausage and brown in a frying pan, once this is completed, strain the sausage and place into a roasting pan.

2. Mix in a saucepan oregano, brown sugar, onion, ketchup and whiskey and bring it to a simmer and stir periodically for 60 minutes.

3. Spoon the sauce mixture on the sausages that are in the roasting pan and mix. Put the roasting pan in the oven at 325 F uncovered and bake for 40minutes.

5) Whiskey Stout Yam Waffles

Waffles is like breakfast any time of day, ensure that you top your batch with some rich maple syrup.

Yield: 6

Cooking Time: 35 minutes

List of Ingredients:

- Baking Powder (1 tbsp.)
- Eggs (3)
- Yams (1 cup, cooked, mashed)
- Flour (1 ½ cups)
- Salt (½ tsp.)
- Milk (½ cup)
- Butter (2 tbsp., melted)
- Stout (½ cup)
- Whiskey (2 tbsp.)
- Pinch of Nutmeg
- Pinch of Ginger

sssssssssssssssssssssssssssssssssssssssssssssss

Methods:

1. Sift the baking powder, flour and salt

2. In a bowl beat the eggs yolks and mix with milk, whiskey, stout, yams, spices and melted butter.

3. Beat the egg whites into the batter

4. Cook with waffle maker and pour maple syrup

5. Serve & Enjoy

6) Filet Mignon with Sweet Whiskey-Coffee Sauce

An amazing meal prepared right in your own kitchen. No need to visit a fancy restaurant, get the same savory burst of flavors right in the comforts of your home.

Yield: 4

Cooking Time: 40 minutes

List of Ingredients:

- Olive Oil cooking spray
- Sugar (1 ½ tsp.)
- Instant Coffee (½ tsp.)
- Salt (¼ tsp.)
- Black pepper (½ tsp.)
- Water (½ cup)
- Parsley (2 tbsp.)
- Whiskey (3 tbsp.)
- Beef –flavored bouillon (½ tsp.)
- Beef Tenderloin Steaks (4 ounces, trimmed)

sss

Methods:

1. Mix salt, pepper, sugar, instant coffee and whiskey in a bowl

2. Season the steak by sprinkling pepper and salt on both sides. Place a skillet on medium heat and cover with olive oil cooking spray.

3. Cook the steak in the pan on either side for 10 minutes

4. Place the Whiskey mixture with beef bouillon in a pan for 3 minutes, until simmer

5. Plate the steak and pour the Whiskey mixture on top and sprinkle with parsley.

6. Serve & Enjoy!

7) Whiskey Bread Pudding

This soft textured bread pudding is guaranteed to be a great addition to any dessert selection. The whiskey sauce gives it just the right tangy touch and it may be topped with whipped cream.

Yield: 4

Cooking Time: 80 minutes

List of Ingredients:

For Whiskey Sauce

- Butter (¼ lb.)
- Bourbon Whiskey (2 tbsp.)
- Sugar (½ cup)
- Water (2 tbsp.)

For Bread Pudding

- French Bread (6oz)
- Butter (1 tbsp.)
- Egg (1)
- Sugar (¾ cup sugar)

- Silvered almonds (2 tbsp.)
- Vanilla Extract (1/8 tsp.)
- Raisins (2 tbsp.)
- Milk (2cups)

sssssssssssssssssssssssssssssssssssssssssssss

Methods:

1. Set oven to 300F/150C

2. In a pan, mix sugar, egg, vanilla extract and milk

3. Set the bread pieces in a baking pan and cover with raisins, pour the mixture to cover the bread and place in oven for 50mins

4. Prepare the whiskey sauce but combining in a saucepan sugar, butter and whiskey and heat until the mixture are blended correctly.

5. Remove the bread pudding from the oven and pour the whiskey sauce on top and serve while warm.

8) Whiskey Corn Chowder

Creamy Corn Chowder mixed with a little Whiskey is guranteed to set any adult gathering as a hit. Add umph to this delicious chowder that will become a new fave.

Yield: 4 cups

Cooking Time: 30 minutes

List of Ingredients:

- Onions (1, diced)
- Nutmeg (¼ tsp., grated)
- Hot Red Pepper (2-3 drops)
- Heavy Cream (½ cup)
- Unsalted Butter (4 tbsp.)
- Canned creamed corn (2 ½ cups)
- Salt (1 tsp.)
- Ground black pepper (1 tsp.)
- Chicken Stock (½ cup)
- Whiskey (¼ cup)

ssssssssssssssssssssssssssssssssssssssssssss

Methods:

1. Melt the butter in a saucepan over medium heat, add onions and then the corn and stir for 5 minutes.

2. Place Whiskey in another saucepan and let it flame for a minute

3. Pour the flaming whiskey into the corn mixture, mix in nutmeg, salt, pepper, heavy cream, chicken stock and hot sauce

4. Once heated thoroughly pour and serve

9) Chocolate Waffles with Whiskey Butter Sauce

What goes great with chocolate? Butter sauce, this flavor full whiskey butter sauce will give you just the right start to any morning breakfast or brunch.

Yield: 6

Cooking Time: 40 minutes

List of Ingredients:

For Butter Sauce

- Brown Sugar (1/3 cup)
- Whiskey (¼ cup)
- Egg (1)
- Vanilla Extract (1 tsp.)
- Butter (4 tbsp.)

For Waffles

- All-purpose Flour (1 ½ cups)
- Baking Powder (2 tsp.)
- Milk (2 cups)
- Eggs (2)
- Cocoa Powder (½ cup, unsweetened)
- Salt (¼ tsp.)
- Vanilla Extract (1 tsp.)
- Butter (4 tbsp., melted)
- Baking Soda (½ tsp.)
- Sugar (¼, granulated)
- Chocolate Chips or Walnuts (½ cup)

sssssssssssssssssssssssssssssssssssssssssss

Methods:

1. Combine flour, sugar, baking powder, baking soda, salt and cocoa powder (dry ingredients) and milk, eggs and vanilla (wet ingredients). Whisk together and let is set of 20mins

2. Set the waffle maker as desired, mix chocolate chips/walnuts and melted butter into the waffle mixture until texture is smooth.

3. Once the waffle maker is at the desired heat pour the batter in approximately ¼ cup and continue this step until the batter is done, set aside all the waffles.

4. In a saucepan mix vanilla, sugar, butter and salt over a low heat. Crack and egg in a separate bowl and whisk it into the butter and sugar mixture. Continue to stir for 5 minutes until the mixture thickens.

5. Plate the waffles and pour the butter mixture on top. Serve & Enjoy!

10) Whiskey Soda Bread

Sweet savory bread stuffed with Whiskey-soaked raisins and orange rind, tantilizing and soft fluffy soda bread is greatly paired with a butter cream.

Yield: 10

Cooking Time: 60 minutes

List of Ingredients:

- Whiskey (1 1/8 cup)
- Sugar (½ cup)
- Salt (1 tsp.)
- Baking Soda (½ tsp.)
- Margarine (¾ butter, melted)
- Orange Rind (1 tbsp., grated)
- Buttermilk (1 1/3 cups)
- All-purpose flour (3 cups)
- Baking Powder (1 tbsp.)
- Raisins (1 cup)

sssssssssssssssssssssssssssssssssssssssssss

Methods:

1. Soak raisins in Whiskey overnight

2. In a bowl mix sugar, salt, flour, baking powder and orange rind

3. Pour in soaked raisins mixture and blend well

4. Soak baking soda in buttermilk, add flour and stir well

5. Pour the mixed batter in a baking pan and bake for 50 minutes

6. Once completed cut in squares and serve

11) Whiskey Burgers

For a great lunch treat or small party, these whiskey burgers are bound to get things started. Mix some freshly squeezed lemonade and enjoy.

Yield: 4

Cooking Time: 65 minutes

List of Ingredients:

- Hamburger Buns
- Whiskey (¼ cup)
- Butter (2 tbsp., melted)
- Salt (½ tsp.)
- Scallions (2/3 cup, diced)
- Ground Beef (1 lb.)
- Barbecue Sauce (½ cup)
- Red Pepper (¼ tsp., minced)
- Ground Pork (1 lb.)
- Garlic (4 cloves, crushed)
- Bread Crumbs (¼ cup)
- Ground black pepper (¼ tsp.)

- Worcestershire Sauce (2 ½ tbsp.)
- Lettuce, Onion and Tomato (sliced)
- Cheddar Cheese (2 cups, sliced)

sssssssssssssssssssssssssssssssssssssssssssssss

Methods:

1. Mix together 1/3 onion, 1/3 whiskey, 2 crushed garlic, bread crumbs, melted butter, salt, red pepper, ground pepper, Worcestershire sauce, ground pork and ground beef. Use this mixture to form the burger patties

2. Set grill at medium heat and grill the patties for 10mins or either side

3. Spread barbecue sauce on hamburger buns, place the burger patty and include desired toppings (onions, lettuce, tomato, cheddar cheese).

12) Honey- Whiskey Chicken Wings

If you are having small dinner party or a movie night, these honey-whiskey chicken wings are sure to start things of right. Grab a couple beers and Enjoy!

Yield: 12

Cooking Time: 60 minutes

List of Ingredients:

- Honey (¾ cup)
- Dijon Mustard (¼ cup)
- Lime Zest (2 tbsp., grated)
- Whiskey (¼ cup)
- Sugar (2 tbsp.)
- Ancho Chili Powder (2 tbsp.)
- Chicken Wings (2 dozen)
- Salt & Pepper

sssssssssssssssssssssssssssssssssssssssssssss

Methods:

1. Set oven to 450F

2. Place the wings on a baking sheet and season with salt and pepper

3. Roast in oven for 40 minutes until golden brown

4. In a saucepan on medium heat add honey, mustard and whiskey and bring to a simmer.

5. Mix sugar with lime zest, chili powder and 1 ½ tsp. of salt

6. Put the wings in a bowl and pour the whiskey sauce on top

7. Once coated, drizzle with the sugar mixture

8. Serve & Enjoy!

13) Whiskey Marinated Steak with Chimichurri Sauce

For a fancy meal look towards this whiskey marinated steak topped with a mixture of herbs and spices into the Chimichurri Sauce. Filling and tasty once prepared correctly the juices from the steak alone could do the trick but top with the sauce and it's a match made in heaven.

Yield: 8

Cooking Time: 50 minutes

List of Ingredients:

- Whiskey (2 tbsp.)
- Olive Oil (¼ cup)
- Ground black pepper (¼ tsp.)
- Honey (2 tbsp.)
- Salt (2 tsp.)
- Skirt Steak (2 ½ lbs.)
- Chimichurri Sauce
- Cilantro (½ cup, crushed)
- Oregano (1 tbsp., crushed)
- Lemon Juice (¼ cup)
- Water (¼ cup)
- Parsley (½ cup, crushed)
- Red Onion (¼ cup, crushed)
- Garlic (3 cloves, crushed)
- Red Wine Vinegar (¼ cup)
- Extra Virgin Olive Oil (2 tbsp.)

ssssssssssssssssssssssssssssssssssssssssssssss

Methods:

1. Mix together, 1/8 tsp. black pepper, ½ tsp. salt, honey, whiskey olive oil, soy sauce, place the skirt steak along with the mixture in a Ziploc bag and marinated overnight.

2. Mix together all the ingredients for the Chimichurri Sauce and set aside in refrigerator for one hour.

3. Sprinkle olive oil on the grill and cook the marinate steak on either side for 4 minutes (2 minutes for medium rare)

4. Let the steak rest for 5 minutes before slicing.

5. Pour the refrigerated Chimichurri Sauce over steak and serve.

14) Cheddar Whiskey Fondue

A touch of Whiskey will give this rich cheddar fondue a highland fling, it is easy and fast to make just using a few ingredients.

Yield: 6

Cooking Time: 20 minutes

List of Ingredients:

- Butter (1 tbsp.)
- Extra Sharp Cheddar Cheese (1 lb., grated)
- Sweet Onion (1 cup, crushed)
- Milk (1 cup)
- Cornstarch (1 tbsp.)
- Whiskey (¼ cup)

sssssssssssssssssssssssssssssssssssssssssssss

Methods:

1. Sauté onions in a saucepan over medium heat in butter until soft

2. Pour in milk and bring the pot to a simmer

3. Include the cheddar cheese and mix until the cheese is melted and smooth

4. In a bowl, combine cornstarch and Whiskey stir until smooth

5. While mixing the cheddar mixture in the saucepan, slowly pour in the Whiskey mixture and stir until texture is thick.

6. Pour Cheddar Whiskey Fondue in a fondue pot and serve

15) Butternut Squash Gnocchi with Whiskey Cream Sauce

For gluten free low fat creamy entrée the butternut squash will provide, any salty, sour craving one might be having. This may be served with crescent rolls and a glass of lemonade.

Yield: 4

Cooking Time: 75 minutes

List of Ingredients:

- Salt (1 tsp.)
- Ground black pepper (1 tsp.)
- Butternut Squash (1 lb.)
- Bourbon Whiskey (1 cup)
- Nutmeg/Cinnamon/Ginger (¾ tsp.)
- Eggs (2)
- Butter (3 tbsp.)
- Shallots (2, sliced)
- Chicken stock (2 cups)
- Garlic (4 cloves, crushed)
- Flour (2 ¼ cups)
- Parmesan Cheese (½ cup)
- Heavy Cream (1/3 cup)
- Thyme for Garnish

ssssssssssssssssssssssssssssssssssssssssssssss

Methods:

1. Set the oven to 450F. Cut and remove the seeds, puree the flesh of the squash in a food processor until smooth

2. Combine eggs, salt, pepper, nutmeg, pureed squash and parmesan cheese with flour and work the mix in with your hands.

3. Sprinkle flour on counter top and baking paper, form a long strip out of the dough and slice the strip into small bits.

4. Boil the gnocchi in batches for 5 minutes each set or until they float to the top.

5. Stir butter and flour over a large pan on medium heat, include garlic and shallot and continue to mix for 3 minutes. After which add the whiskey and chicken stock.

6. Continue to mix until the mixture is thin, lower the heat and pour the heavy cream, salt and pepper.

7. Once all the gnocchi are completed add them to the cream mixture and mix to fully coat.

8. Plate, garnish and serve.

16) Whiskey Barbecue Sauce

This Whiskey Barbecue sauce is a crowds favorite, which is mostly used in resturants but the best part is that it is easy to make at home. Goes well with Chicken, Pork and Beef

Yield: 3 cups

Cooking Time: 10 minutes

List of Ingredients:

- Olive Oil (1 tbsp.)
- Garlic (2 cloves, minced)
- Ketchup (1 cup)
- Dry Mustard (1 tsp.)
- Lemon Juice (2 tbsp.)
- Soy Sauce (1 tbsp. on)
- Butter (1 tbsp.)
- Onion (2 cups, diced)
- Molasses (½ cup)
- Red Wine Vinegar (¼ cup)
- Ground Black Pepper (¼ tsp.)
- Lemon Zest (½ tsp.)

- Paprika (1 tbsp.)
- Whiskey (1/3 cup)

sssssssssssssssssssssssssssssssssssssssssssss

Methods:

1. Melt butter with oil in a saucepan over medium heat, sauté the onions and garlic for 2 minutes.

2. Mix Ketchup, Vinegar, Paprika, Molasses, Lemon Juice, Pepper, Mustard, Soy Sauce, Lemon Zest and Whiskey

3. Stir into sautéed mixture, bring to a boil, cover and let it simmer for 35 minutes

4. After cooling you may refrigerate in a tightly sealed container.

17) Bourbon Whiskey Salmon

This classy dish could be served with a whiskey cocktail and roasted asparagus

Yield: 4

Cooking Time: 60 minutes

List of Ingredients:

- Bourbon Whiskey (¼ cup)
- Brown Sugar (2 tbsp.)
- Lime Juice (1 tbsp.)
- Garlic (2 cloves, crushed)
- Salmon Fillets (6oz)
- Soy Sauce (3 tbsp.)
- Honey (2 tbsp.)
- Ginger (1 tbsp., crushed)
- Black Pepper (½ tsp.)
- Sesame Seeds or Green Onions to Garnish

sssssssssssssssssssssssssssssssssssssssssss

Methods:

1. Add whiskey, brown sugar, lime juice, garlic, soy sauce, honey, ginger and black pepper in a Ziploc bag and marinated the Salon fillets for 40minutes.

2. Set the oven to 425F, lay parchment paper, aluminum foil and cooking spray

3. Lay the Salmon on the sheet and cover with a little of the marinade, bake for 7 minutes flip the salmon cover with marinade once more and bake for 7 minutes again.

4. Remove the Salmon and plate, sprinkle with green onions and/or sesame seeds

18) Chocolate Whiskey Balls

What a treat! These small chocolate whiskey balls would make great appetizer for any small get together the famiy would be having, whether as a treat before the main course or after, it's a burst of delight.

Yield: 24-36

Cooking Time: 30 minutes

List of Ingredients:

- Chocolate Wafer Cookie Crumbs (1 cup)
- Light Corn Syrup (1 tbsp.)
- Pecans (1 cup)
- Sugar (1 cup)
- Whiskey (¼ cup)
- Powdered sugar to roll

sssssssssssssssssssssssssssssssssssssssssss

Methods:

1. Place in a food processor chocolate wafers and pecans, grind and empty the content from the processor into a bowl.

2. Add sugar, Whiskey and corn syrup to the bowl

3. Mix thoroughly with hands and shape the dough into small balls.

4. Store balls in Ziploc bag in the refrigerator until firm

5. Remove after 20 minutes and Serve!

19) Coconut Butter Whiskey Snowballs

These snowballs made with coconut, walnuts, whiskey and nutmeg will be a burst of delight and like a holiday as come to life.

Yield: 4

Cooking Time: 60 minutes

List of Ingredients:

- Bourbon Whiskey (½ cup)
- Vanilla Extract (1 tsp.)
- Walnuts (1 cup, diced)
- Medjool Dates (6, pitted)
- Shredded Coconut (3 cups)
- Nutmeg (1 tsp.)

sssssssssssssssssssssssssssssssssssssssssss

Methods:

1. For 15 minutes soak dates in whiskey

2. While the dates soak, prepare the covering by putting 2 ½ cups of coconut in a food processor and process until smooth, ensure all pieces are processed.

3. Add the soaked dates to the processor along with 2 tbsp. of whiskey, nutmeg and vanilla, process again.

4. Include walnuts to the mixture and pulse until mixture is soft enough to create balls

5. Once the balls are created refrigerate for 1 hour

6. Sprinkle each ball with remaining coconut pieces and serve.

20) Irish Whiskey Potato Green Chile Stew

Add a little Mexican and Irish mixture to your plate with this Potato Green Chile Stew, which can be paired with tortillas or chips.

Yield: 8

Cooking Time: 2 hours

List of Ingredients:

- Garlic (2 tbsp., diced)
- Jalapenos (2, chopped)
- Tomatoes (2 cups, sliced)
- Potatoes (8, cubed)
- Oregano (1 tbsp.)
- Salt (½ tbsp.)
- Black Pepper (1 tbsp.)
- Beef Broth (8 cups)
- Onions (2 cups, diced)
- Green Chiles (4 cups, diced)
- Irish whiskey (2 tbsp.)

- Lamb Meat (1 lb., cubed)
- Olive Oil (½ cup)

ssssssssssssssssssssssssssssssssssssssssssssss

Methods:

1. In a medium heat pan sauté onions, garlic, jalapenos, salt, black pepper and oregano in olive oil for 10 minutes

2. Place the lamb meat in the sautéed pan for 15 minutes, add potatoes and pour the whiskey, stir for an additional 10 minutes.

3. Include Green Chiles and Tomatoes to the pan of ingredients and stir until warmed.

4. Pour in the beef broth and simmer for 1 hour.

5. Serve with hot flour tortillas or steamed rice.

21) Cherry Apple Whiskey Sour Popsicles

Fun, chill and relaxing popsicles, these cool frozen treats can be used at any pool party or a small trip to the beach. Easy to make and a health treat you can indulge in.

Yield: 8

Cooking Time: 45 minutes

List of Ingredients:

- Green Apple (1, large)
- Whiskey (1 cup)
- Cherries (3 cups)
- Lime (1, large)
- Lemon Juice (½ cup)
- Water (¼ cup)
- Sugar (¼ cup)

sssssssssssssssssssssssssssssssssssssssssss

Methods:

1. Peel the apples, remove the skin from the lime and pit the cherries. Slice all fruits in quarters

2. Place all the fruits, whiskey, lemon juice, water and sugar in blender and blend until pureed.

3. Place mixture into Popsicle set and freeze until the mixture is solidified.

22) One-Pan Whiskey Flavored Pork Chops

Looking for rich, succulent flavored pork chops for dinner? Look no more this one-pan whiskey flavored pork chops is guaranteed to work any time. Pair with mash potatoes or roasted vegetables and red wine for a perfect combination.

Yield: 4

Cooking Time: 50 minutes

List of Ingredients:

- Water (½ cup)
- Salt (½ tsp.)
- Black Pepper (¼ tsp.)
- Olive Oil (1 tsp.)
- Sour cream (2/3 cup, fat free)
- Flour (2 tbsp.)
- Rubbed Sage (½ tsp.)
- Bone-in Pork Chops (6 ounce, trimmed)
- Onion (½ cups, diced)
- Mushrooms (8 ounce, pre-sliced)

- Whiskey (½ cup)

ssssssssssssssssssssssssssssssssssssssssssssssss

Methods:

1. Set oven at 300F

2. Mix Sour cream, Water, All-purpose flour, Salt, Rubbed Sage and Black Pepper in a bowl

3. Cover each side of the pork chops with salt and pepper.

4. Warm the oil in a skillet over medium heat

5. Sauté Pork chops for 6 minutes on both sides

6. Remove pork chops from the pan and stir fry onions and mushrooms for 3 minutes

7. Slowly pour the whiskey in the pan and stir until almost all the liquid is evaporated.

8. Add sour cream mixture and return the pork chops. Stir in the pan and cover for 3 minutes

9. Plate and Serve immediately

23) Whiskey Candied Bacon Deviled Eggs

Deviled eggs are a crowd favorite so at your next dinner party impress guests with this spikes delicacies. They surely won't be disappointed.

Yield: 4

Cooking Time: 60 minutes

List of Ingredients:

- Mayonnaise (¾ cup)
- Maple Syrup (5 tbsp.)
- Chipotle Powder (1 tsp.)
- Hard boiled eggs (12)
- Dijon Mustard (3 tbsp.)
- Black pepper (¼ tsp.)
- Bacon (1 lb., thick- sliced)
- Salt (½ tsp.)
- Light brown sugar (½ cup)
- Whiskey (2 tbsp.)
- Chives

sss

Methods:

1. Set oven to 350 F

2. Layer the baking pan with tin foil

3. Combine sugar, maple syrup, Dijon mustard, whiskey salt and chipotle powder.

4. Coat the slices of bacon and place each stripe on the tin foil

5. Bake until bacon is crispy and caramelized. Dice the stripes and set aside.

6. Slice the hard boiled eggs in half and remove the yolk

7. Combine the yolks with mayonnaise, Dijon mustard, maple syrup, black pepper, chipotle powder and a few bits of the bacon

8. Place the mixture back in the middle of the egg slices.

9. Garnish with chives and pieces of the bacon.

24) Whiskey Fudge Brownies

What a fun treat? Easy and fun to make, after the main course this would make a nice treat with a glass of wine. These brownies could make good party favors or appetizers.

Yield: 20

Cooking Time: 40 minutes

List of Ingredients:

- Olive Oil cooking spray
- Chocolate Chips (¼ cup)
- Unsweetened Cocoa (½ cup)
- Salt (½ tsp.)
- Vanilla Extract (½ tsp.)
- All-purpose flour (1 ½ cups)
- Baking Powder (1 tsp.)
- Sugar (1 1/3 cups)
- Butter (6 tbsp., melted)
- Eggs (2, large)
- Whiskey (¼ cup)

sssssssssssssssssssssssssssssssssssssssssssss

Methods:

1. Set oven at 350F

2. Boil the Whiskey in a saucepan, remove from stove and mix in chocolate chips until smooth

3. Mix in a bowl Baking powder, cocoa, flour and salt

4. Beat with a mixer sugar, butter, vanilla, eggs, flour mixture and Whiskey mixture

5. Spread the mixture in a square baking pan sprayed with olive oil cooking spray.

6. Bake for 30minutes

7. Cool, Cut and Serve.

25) Grilled Chicken with Whiskey-Ginger Marinade

Delicious main course, easy to make and will be enjoyed by the whole family, may be served with rice or roasted potatoes.

Yield: 4

Cooking Time: 60 minutes

List of Ingredients:

- Soy Sauce (1/3 cup)
- Hoisin sauce (2 tbsp.)
- Lime Juice (2 tbsp.)
- Ginger (2 tsp., grated)
- Red Pepper (¼ tsp., minced)
- Olive Oil cooking spray
- Cornstarch (½ tsp.)
- Brown Sugar (3 tbsp.)
- Sesame Oil (2 tsp.)
- Garlic (2 cloves, crushed)
- Water (1 tbsp.)
- Sesame Seeds (1 tsp., toasted)
- Boneless Chicken Breasts (1 ounce, boneless)
- Whiskey (1/3 cup)

sssssssssssssssssssssssssssssssssssssssssssss

Methods:

1. Wrap each chicken breast with plastic wrap and pound until the meat is ½ inch thick

2. Mix Whiskey, Soy sauce, Hoisin sauce, Lime Juice, Ginger, Red Pepper, Brown Sugar, Sesame Oil and Garlic. Place the chicken breast in a Ziploc bag and pour the marinade on the stripes. Leave refrigerated for one hour.

3. Warm up the grill and remove the marinade meat from the refrigerator.

4. Spray the cooking spray on the grill, each chicken stripe should be grilled for five minutes.

5. Once all stripes are completed, place on a platter and slice thinly

6. Boil water, cornstarch and the marinade mix, leave to simmer for 10 minutes.

7. Pour the mixture over the chicken stripes and sprinkle sesame seeds

8. Serve & Enjoy!

About the Author

Allie Allen developed her passion for the culinary arts at the tender age of five when she would help her mother cook for their large family of 8. Even back then, her family knew this would be more than a hobby for the young Allie and when she graduated from high school, she applied to cooking school in London. It had always been a dream of the young chef to study with some of Europe's best and she made it happen by attending the Chef Academy of London.

After graduation, Allie decided to bring her skills back to North America and open up her own restaurant. After 10 successful years as head chef and owner, she decided to sell her business and pursue other career avenues. This monumental decision led Allie to her true calling, teaching. She also started to write e-books for her students to study at home for practice. She is now the proud author of several e-books and gives private and semi-private cooking lessons to a range of students at all levels of experience.

Stay tuned for more from this dynamic chef and teacher when she releases more informative e-books on cooking and baking in the near future. Her work is infused with stores and anecdotes you will love!

Author's Afterthoughts

I can't tell you how grateful I am that you decided to read my book. My most heartfelt thanks that you took time out of your life to choose my work and I hope you find benefit within these pages.

There are so many books available today that offer similar content so that makes it even more humbling that you decided to buying mine.

Tell me what you thought! I am eager to hear your opinion and ideas on what you read as are others who are looking for a good book to buy. Leave a review on Amazon.com so others can benefit from your wisdom!

With much thanks,

Allie Allen

Printed in Great Britain
by Amazon